Contents

		Page
1	Hanged for Murder	1
2	The Case of Dr Crippen	5
3	The Brides in the Bath Murders	12
4	The Face of Murder	21
5	The Hangman's Noose	26

Peter Falk plays Columbo, the policeman in the TV series. He always makes sure the murderer ends up behind bars.

Hanged for
Murder

John Townsend

Published in association with The Basic Skills Agency

Hodder & Stoughton

A MEMBER OF THE HODDER HEADLINE GROUP

Acknowledgements
Cover artwork: Dave Smith
Illustration: Dave Hopkins
Photos: p. 1 © Ronald Grant Archive; pp. 7, 10, 19 © Hulton Getty; pp. 14, 22, 23 © Public Record Office Image Library.

Every effort has been made to trace copyright holders of material reproduced in this book. Any rights not acknowledged will be acknowledged in subsequent printings if notice is given to the printer.

Orders: please contact Bookpoint Ltd, 130 Milton Park, Abingdon, Oxon OX14 4SB. Telephone: (44) 01235 827720, Fax: (44) 01235 400454. Lines are open from 9.00 – 6.00, Monday to Saturday, with a 24 hour message answering service. Email address: orders@bookpoint.co.uk

British Library Cataloguing in Publication Data
A catalogue record for this title is available from The British Library

ISBN 0 340 84859 6

First published 2002
Impression number   10 9 8 7 6 5 4 3 2 1
Year   2007 2006 2005 2004 2003 2002

Typeset by SX Composing DTP, Rayleigh, Essex.
Printed in Great Britain for Hodder & Stoughton Educational, a division of Hodder Headline Plc, 338 Euston Road, London NW1 3BH by The Bath Press Ltd.

1 Hanged for Murder

Tales of killers seem to grip us in a spell.
The murder plot holds us in its power.
From the first stories ever told –
to last night's TV cop shows.
We all like a mystery.
We all like to find out the truth.
And we always want to know
the answers to the same questions:

- Who did it?
- How did they kill?
- Why?

And the biggest question of all:
Will the killer get caught?

There's nothing like seeing
a villain come to a bad end!

Yet, if a murderer wants to get away with it,
there are always two big problems:
1) How to hide the body.
2) How to cover up all the clues.

There must be no clues left
to point to the killer.
But is there such a thing
as a perfect murder?

For those who try to solve murders,
it can be a huge task.
They must find the killer's one mistake.
They must hunt for every piece of the jigsaw.
But can they crack the puzzle?
It's all down to finding just a shred of proof.
The stories in this book
are all about just that – proof.
And these stories are proof that crime doesn't pay.

With all the hi-tech help from computers today,
the police may have an easier job.
But what about many years ago?
Which crimes from long ago
changed police work forever?

Many of the murder cases from the past
make good reading.
There is plenty of mystery
to give us a shiver of fear.
But they also teach us about the past.

In this book, there are three cases
where the killers almost got away with murder.
They all thought they were clever.
They all thought they were safe.
But instead, they became victims of death
themselves – victims of the noose.
All three cases ended in hanging.

You might see them today as wax works
in museums of murder . . .
if you dare to meet them face to face.
The killers were all hanged in the last century.
These true stories raise questions about
the whole subject of hanging for murder.

The death penalty was used for centuries in Britain.
Many people were pleased to see it
go for good in Britain in 1969.

But some would like to see it come back.
From time to time, MPs vote on the subject.
Now and again, people debate
the rights and wrongs of hanging.
After a murderer is sent to prison,
people up and down the land will argue.
Some will say: 'Bring back hanging!'
Others say hanging is wrong.
Many people were hanged but
later found to be innocent.

In 1964, the last two men were hanged in Britain.
The last woman to be hanged in Britain
was Ruth Ellis in 1955.
People still argue that this was wrong.
Some of the proof against the people hanged
was open to question.
These were the days before DNA testing.
It is likely that innocent people
went to the gallows.

You must make up your own mind
in the three chilling cases that follow.

2　The Case of Dr Crippen

Dr Crippen lived in Holloway, London
with his bossy wife, Cora.
Cora would nag him into doing all the chores.
He was a meek little man who did as he was told.

The couple met in New York
and came to London in 1910.
She was an actress and wanted
a glamorous lifestyle.
She couldn't get work in London
but liked to make out that she was a star.
All her jewels and fine clothes cost a fortune.
She told Crippen he had to earn more money.
In the end, they had to take in lodgers
to help pay all of her bills.

Cora loved to nag her husband
in front of the lodgers.
She made him look a fool.

But he had his own secret.
He was in love with a young woman called Ethel.
When Cora found out, she made a big scene.
His life became even more of a misery.
He could take no more.
His plan began on the winter's night
of 31st January 1910.

The Crippens had friends round to dinner.
It was the last time Cora was seen alive.
A few days later, Crippen sold some of her jewels.
He told people she had gone back to the USA
to see a dying sister.
No one asked too many questions – at first.
But when Ethel moved in with him,
some eye-brows were raised.
Or was she just another lodger?

It soon became clear what was going on.
The gossip spread like wild fire.
But Crippen told friends that Cora was very ill.
He took Ethel away on holiday to France.
When they came back, he calmly told
all of Cora's friends that his dear wife
had sadly died in Los Angeles.

The glamorous Cora Crippen.

People talked.

How could the doctor carry on so calmly?

And why was Ethel wearing Cora's furs and jewels?

It all seemed a bit strange.

But then the tongues really did start to wag.

One of Cora's friends came back from Los Angeles.

There was no truth in the story

that Cora Crippen had died there.

The police went knocking on Dr Crippen's door.

Crippen told the police his wife

was not really dead.

He told them he made up the story

of her death because of his shame.

She had run off with another man.

The police felt sorry for him and went away.

The police came back a few days later.

The house was empty. Crippen had left in a hurry.

After three days of searching the house,

the police found Cora's body under the cellar floor.

But the body had been cut up.

The head, arms and legs were cut off.

They took away the grisly remains to the labs.

They found that the cause of death was poison.

The news hit the world by storm.
Where were Crippen and Ethel?
The hunt was on.
Little did anyone know
they were on board ship on the way to Canada.
Ethel was dressed as a boy and
Crippen had shaved his moustache.
Even so, the ship's captain knew who they were.
He had to tell the police back in London.

The ship had a new radio on board.
It used morse code.
The captain sent his message
and the police were on their way
– on a faster ship.
This was the first time a radio
was used to catch a murderer.

Dr Crippen: hanged for murder.

Crippen and Ethel were about to leave the ship.
A policeman dressed as a pilot called after them.
'Dr Crippen?'

Without thinking, the doctor turned.
'Yes?'

'So it is you! You are under arrest for murder.'

The trial at the Old Bailey drew huge crowds.
The little doctor stayed calm and gentle.
One witness said he was a very nice man.
But the verdict soon came – GUILTY.

Dr Crippen met his death by the rope
in November 1910.
Ethel went to live in Canada.
She took a note from Crippen with her.
It said 'Death has no terror for me.'
His story lives on long after those last words.

3 The Brides in the Bath Murders

It was a cold night, just a week
before Christmas in 1914.
The landlady ran a hot bath for her new lodger
and went back downstairs to her ironing.
She heard splashes from the bathroom upstairs.
Her new lodgers seemed a nice couple.
They had only been married for two days.
John had gone out to get some supper
for his new wife, Margaret – while she took a bath.

As the landlady put down her iron,
she thought she heard a thud upstairs.
Then the doorbell rang.
It was John Lloyd coming home with their supper.
He went upstairs but was soon shouting,
'Come and help. She's in the bath.'

His wife lay still in the bath.
Her face was under the water.
He tried to lift her out and give her the kiss of life
while the landlady ran for help.
By the time a doctor came it was too late.
Margaret Lloyd was dead.

The doctor had seen Margaret Lloyd
only the day before when John took her to see him.
She had been having dizzy spells.
Maybe it was the start of flu.
It seemed the hot bath made her pass out
and she drowned.
The *News of the World* told the story:
'BRIDE'S TRAGIC FATE
ON DAY AFTER WEDDING.'
It was a sad story and people felt so sorry
for poor John Lloyd.
His new love had come to such a tragic end.

OLIVER.GEORGE.LOVE   1107   9.11.1900

John Lloyd had other wives and other names.
Here his name was Oliver Love.

No one knew that John Lloyd was not his real name.
No one knew that he had other wives.
No one knew that only the day before she died
Margaret had made a will and insured her life
for a lot of money.
John Lloyd would now be rich.

No one knew all these facts.
But the story in the *News of the World*
made someone sit up and think.
Someone many miles away wrote a letter
to Scotland Yard. He smelt a rat.
He was the father of Alice –
who had died a year ago, just after
her wedding to George Smith.
She had died in her bath.

The police said that they would look into the story.
They soon found out that Alice had died
in just the same way as Margaret.
Both died in their bath –
with no sign of a struggle.
Both were found by their husband.
Both saw their doctor only the day before.
Both had just made a will
– leaving every penny to their husband.
It all looked very fishy.
The police now had to find out more.
Could John Lloyd be the same man as George Smith?

The police took John Lloyd to the police station.
They asked, 'Have you been married before?'

'No.'

'Have you ever changed your name?'

'No.'

Then the police brought in Alice's father.
He looked at John Lloyd long and hard.
He looked right into his eyes.
'That's him. There's no doubt about it.
That's George Smith. He married my daughter Alice.
He killed my girl!'

George Smith was his real name.
The police began to find out a lot about him.
He was born in 1872.
He had been in the army but went to prison for theft.
He had many girlfriends but also many wives.
He had cheated most of them
and ran off with all of their money.

In 1912, George Smith had married Bessie.
She was rich so he had made her write a will.

If she died, he would get all her money.
You can guess the rest!

Smith took his new wife to the doctor
the day after they got married.
He said she had fits.
The next day he ran back to the doctor.
'Come at once. My wife is dead in the bath.'
It looked as though she had had a fit and drowned.
Of course, he got to keep all her money.

So now the police knew they had their man.
But they still had a problem.
How could they prove that George Smith had
killed all the victims?
After all, the doctors had all said
there was no sign of a struggle.
Each of the wives had died by fainting in the bath.

The police took the tin bath away
to the police station. They did many tests.
How could anyone drown in such a small tub?
There was no way anyone's head
could be pushed right under.
So how could they prove she had been killed?

The police asked a woman of Margaret's size
to sit in the bath tub.
They filled it with warm water.
There was no way her head could be
pushed under the water.
Unless . . .

A policeman suddenly took hold of her feet
and pulled.
She slid forward and her head fell back.
Down she went and her head went right under fast.
She began to pass out.
They had to pull her out quick.
So that was it – that's how he did it!

George Joseph Smith was charged with murder.
He went on trial at The Old Bailey in June 1915.
Crowds came to watch.
They all wanted to see this man
who had cast a spell over so many women.
The trial lasted nine days.
The judge then took three hours to sum up.
The jury didn't take long to make up its mind.
How did it find George Smith?
GUILTY.

George Smith with his wife, Bessie Mundy. He murdered
Bessie in 1912.

Friday 13th is thought to be unlucky for some.
It was for George Smith.
On Friday 13th August 1915,
he was led up to the gallows.
While other men were dying for king and country,
in World War I, George Smith was to die for
his abuse of women.
They hanged him at Maidstone Prison.

George Smith had married seven times.
He drowned three of his wives
– but the insurance money was no good to him now.
Nor was all the money he took from
his other wives before he deserted them.
Women all over the country despised him.

The rope was put round his neck,
the hood went over his head
and the trap door flew open.
He fell to his death and became one of
the most hated killers to be hanged in England.
The case of The Brides in the Bath Murders
has been talked about ever since.

4 The Face of Murder

The first face in Britain to be 'made-up'
from a kit was that of Edwin Bush.
The police used the new IDENTI-KIT
to ask the public: 'Have you seen this man?'
And it worked.

Bush went into an antique shop in London in 1961.
He saw a sword in the window
and went in to ask how much it was.
He saw a way to make quick money.
He could buy the sword and sell it for a profit
in a gun shop nearby.

The next day Edwin Bush went back
to the antique shop.
He asked the woman behind the counter
if he could see the sword.
There was no one else in the shop.

The antique shop in London where Edmund Bush committed the murder of Elsie Batten.

Bush grabbed a dagger
and stabbed the woman three times.
She fell in a pool of blood
and he ran from the shop, taking the sword.
He ran to the gun shop to sell the sword for £10.

His victim was Elsie Batten.
She was dead when they found her –
with the dagger still in her chest.
The police began a murder hunt.

The owner of the antique shop told
the police about the missing sword.
He told them of the man
who asked about it the day before.
The police made up a picture using
the description and their new kit of faces.

The posters of the 'killer's face'
were sent around London.
Just a few days later, PC Cole
was on his beat in Soho.
He saw a man who looked just like
the face on the poster.

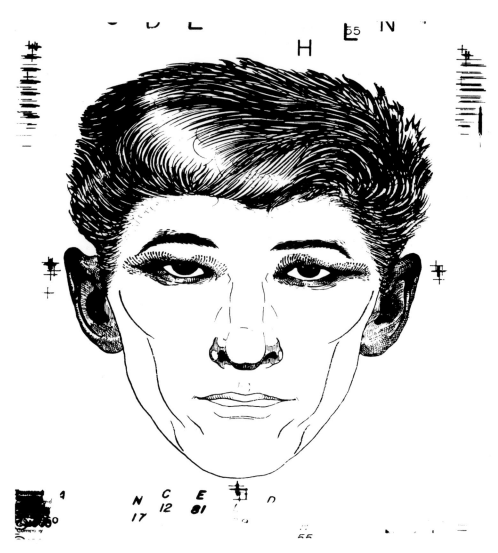

Identi-Kit picture of Edwin Bush.

He went up to the man and arrested him.
It was Edwin Bush.

Bush had left fingerprints on the dagger.
He also had Elsie's blood on his clothes.
There was no doubt that he was the killer.
His trial was at the Old Bailey.

Bush was found guilty and hanged in May 1961.
The police now had another tool
in their hunt for killers.

5   The Hangman's Noose

Hundreds of murder stories from the last century
tell of killers being caught and hanged.
The police found enough clues
to track them down at last.
News of the trials filled the papers.
Crowds packed the courts.
Many cheered when the judge put on the black cap
and looked the killer coldly in the face,
and said, 'You will hang from your neck until dead.'

Hanging for murder has now stopped in Britain.
Was it right or wrong?
What do you think?
How do you feel about these killers
and their victims?

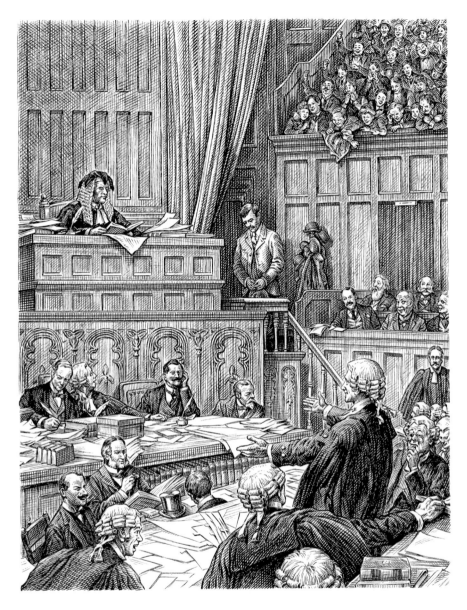

'GUILTY!'

To find out more about these three stories,
you can visit New Scotland Yard's website.
You can see more pictures.
You can read of other murders, too.
You can find more grim details in the crime museum.
Look at:

www.newscotlandyard.police.uk/history/index.htm

You will see that murder doesn't pay.

So . . . sleep well!